Presented to:

_____

With love from:

_____

On:

_____

For Grandma P.
–LD

For Andrea, gone but never forgotten.
–LF

ZONDERKIDZ

How High is Heaven
Copyright © 2022 by Linsey Davis
Illustrations © 2022 by Lucy Fleming

Requests for information should be addressed to:

Zonderkidz, 3900 Sparks Drive, Grand Rapids, Michigan 49546

Hardcover ISBN 978-0-310-77006-0
Ebook ISBN 978-0-310-77007-7

Design and art direction: Cindy Davis

Printed in Korea

22 23 24 25 26 27 / SAM / 21 20 19 18 17 16 15 14 13 12 11 10 9 8 7 6 5 4 3 2 1

How High is Heaven?

Written by
LINSEY DAVIS

Illustrated by Lucy Fleming

How do I get to heaven? There's someone I'd like to see.

My grandma lives there, and every day she's watching over me.

There's so much I'd like to tell her.
I've lots of questions too.
There must be a way to visit her,
but I'm not really sure what to do.

I'll try building a staircase to heaven.
Then climb my way up, brick by brick.
The taller I build it, the higher I'll go.
I think that should do the trick.

I WONDER HOW GRAN GOT TO HEAVEN.
Did God give her wings to fly?

I don't have wings,
but I've got other things.
I guess I'll continue to try.

Could I bounce my way up to heaven, past treetops and clouds up above?

If I jump high enough, will I get to see
the grandma I so dearly love?

How high in the sky is heaven?

Could I go in a hot air balloon?

If I float off today, past the big Milky Way,

will I get to see grandma real soon?

We're taking a trip on an airplane.

This is it! I can hardly wait.

As we fly through the sky, I'm hoping to see
my gran at the big pearly gate.

I heard that heaven is joyful—a beautiful sight to behold.

Where the glory of God shines so brightly
on everyone there, young and old.

But the plane didn't take us to heaven.
We landed in Tucson instead.
And there at the gate was my grandpa,
who planted a kiss on my head.

I sure wish we could visit heaven

and give gran a hug and a smile.

But I'm not quite sure how to get there,
So I'm still stuck on earth for a while.

Then one day at church with my family,
the pastor had something to say.
He talked about getting to heaven.
He told us there's only one way.

It's not about how far you travel,

or not just the things that you do.

It's all about faith and the grace of God
that brings this gift to you.

If we open our hearts to others
and love and believe
in the Lord,

then we'll be living our very best life

and heaven will be our reward.

So, for now I'll keep living this good life that God gave to me at birth.

One day I'll see gran, but until that time ...

I'll enjoy heaven
here on earth.